Captive Christmas

A Comedy in Three Acts

By
Vin Morreale, Jr.

Cover Design by
Mandy Morreale

ISBN 978-1-7347313-6-1

academyartspress.com

All Rights Reserved.
Copyright © 2019 by Vin Morreale, Jr.

Captive Christmas

by
Vin Morreale, Jr.

CAST

One	50, Angry Construction Worker
Two	68, Wino Accountant
Three	39, Female Ad Executive
Four	24, Nerdy Slacker
Five	42, Mild-mannered Counselor
Six	27, Hispanic Taxi Driver
Bernie	31, Deranged Kidnapper

SETTING

A locked basement on Christmas Eve.

FOR ROYALTY INFORMATION AND PERMISSION TO USE THIS PLAY IN A PERFORMANCE, PLEASE EMAIL VIN@ACADEMYARTS.COM

ACT ONE

AT RISE. The curtain remains closed. The stage is in darkness, as offstage voices are heard.

BERNIE. *(Offstage, roughly)* Come on, move it! Through here. Let's go!

FIVE. *(Offstage.)* Look, buddy, I...

BERNIE. *(Offstage.)* I said move it!

FIVE. *(Offstage.)* You're making a big mistake here...

BERNIE. *(Offstage.)* If you don't stop stalling, you ain't never gonna see New Years, capiche?

FIVE. *(Offstage.)* But I'm not...

BERNIE. *(Offstage.)* Capiche?!

FIVE. *(Offstage.)* Uh... yeah. I capiche...

BERNIE. *(Offstage.)* Then move it!

FIVE. *(Offstage.)* I just want to know something.

BERNIE. *(Offstage.)* What's that?

FIVE. *(Offstage.)* Why me?

BERNIE. *(Offstage.)* Maybe I just like the way you dress..

(The two enter through the audience from the back of the theater. BERNIE is a short, stocky man in his early thirties, with a dark hair and sinister expression. He is dressed in a black muscle shirt and sports an erratic haircut that could only be self-inflicted. He is prodding the other man toward the stage with a large pistol in his back. FIVE, his kidnapping victim, stumbles forward, because of his blindfold. He is a mild-mannered man in his early forties dressed like Santa Claus.)

BERNIE. Watch your feet, man!

FIVE. Whatta you expect with this blindfold on?

BERNIE. Any more whining outa you and it's gonna be Silent Night. You hear me?! *(Softening his tone.)* I don't know why you're complaining. You think I like doing this?

FIVE. Excuse me?

BERNIE. You think I like doing this? You think any of this brings me joy?

FIVE. Well, actually...

(They make their way to the front of the stage.)

BERNIE. *(Suddenly angry.)* Well, it don't! If I got caught, what jury in the world is gonna sympathize with a guy who kidnaps street corner Santas on Christmas Eve, huh? Tell me that, huh?!

FIVE. Then why...?

BERNIE. I mean, you kidnap anybody else and you're a big shot terrorist or a hardened criminal. They show your picture on the Nightly News and Entertainment Tonight. You get like twenty-four hour cable news coverage on CNN and 'MS-Hey-Look-At-Me.' Plus you get fan mail and love letters from head cases all over the world.

FIVE. Sounds exciting, but...

BERNIE. I even heard about this guy who's thing was blowing up Porta-Potties. Don't ask me why. After he splatters his tenth Porta-potty, ISIS 'friends' him on Facebook. Talk about your fifteen minutes of fame...

FIVE. I don't even like to use Porta-potties. Really, I...

BERNIE. You're missing the big picture here! It's not about kabooming a tin can crapper. It's about the notoriety. Psycho street cred. Feeding the media beast. Finding your niche among the nutjobs. Standing out in a crowd of crazies. It's not as easy as it sounds, let me tell ya...

FIVE. You have my sympathy. But if you let me...

BERNIE. So Porta-potty boy gets his own fan website...even after that embarrassing premature detonation incident and the thirteen surgeries to remove plastic seat fragments from his face and buttocks. But you just try and swipe a Santa, and everybody thinks something's wrong with you.

(Bernie shoves the nervous Santa forward with the gun.)

BERNIE. That's what you think, ain't it? You think there's something wrong with me, don't you?!

FIVE. Hey, I just...

BERNIE. Damned right you do!

FIVE. Really, I know you're upset about something, but I just want to...

BERNIE. Everyone'd think it was 'cause of my childhood or something. That's what they'd all think.. Like maybe when I was twelve and like my old man mighta put a mousetrap in my Christmas stocking as a joke...

FIVE. A mousetrap?

BERNIE. Hey, I ain't sayin' he did! It's just that, y'know, maybe that's what you might think they'd all be thinking. Or like maybe they'd say my old man mighta gone hunting on Christmas Eve and brought back a deer he shot, tied it up all tight and bloody on the roof of our old station wagon, and y'know, maybe told us kids we was gonna have Donner or Blitzen for Christmas dinner, and us being young and not knowin' any better might've believed him...

FIVE. Donner and Blitzen for dinner...?

BERNIE. I'm not saying he done that either! I'm just saying that's maybe what they'd all think and stuff...Or like some fancy-talkin' psychologist who ain't never even been to reform school might say that maybe my old man could've gift wrapped a hot watch, then kept his mouth shut when they arrested me for possession of stolen goods and I had to spend my entire Christmas vacation in lock-up... (Stops, remembering back.) Man, you should'a seen the look on my Mom's face...

FIVE. Boy, you sure had a rough...

BERNIE. Not that he woulda done any of that! My old man, he was okay, y'know?

FIVE. (Dubiously.) If you say so.

BERNIE. Maybe just a creepy sense of humor is all.

FIVE. No kidding.

BERNIE. *(Suddenly cheerful.)* But enough whining! This is Christmas Eve! *(Growling.)* Get your big red butt in the basement, Santa!

> *(Five turns toward the sound of the man's voice. He tries to sound compassionate and reasonable, despite the quiver of fear in his voice.)*

FIVE. Listen, friend. I'm not the real Santa... and I'm not your father...

BERNIE. Don't you go sayin' nothin' about my old man!

FIVE. Sure, I just...

BERNIE. You hear what I'm saying?!

FIVE. I only meant...

BERNIE. Just don't say nothin' against my Pops, is all!

FIVE. All I meant was... What have you got against me?

BERNIE. *(Suddenly clinical.)* Paranoid schizophrenia which manifests itself in the transference or projection of feelings of hostility toward potentially innocent or otherwise uninvolved people. (Shrugs.) I read that in a book somewhere.

FIVE. Remind me to pick up a copy.

> *(He pushes Five behind the curtain, Stage Left. The loud CLANG of a steel door slamming.)*

BERNIE. *(Offstage.)* Now get in there, elf boy!

> *(The curtain rises to reveal the large concrete cellar into which Bernie has just pushed Five. A heavy steel door Upstage Left. A curtain, Stage Right, provides access to an offstage storage room, offstage. A few broken mannequins lean against the Upstage Wall. Old boxes and yellowed newspapers are scattered throughout.*
>
> *Also scattered throughout are four other people all dressed like Santa. Five removes his blindfold and gapes at the strange assortment of Santa Clauses.)*

FOUR. Welcome to the North Pole!

ONE. Sorry. The job's already taken.

(SANTA ONE is a tall, gruff-looking Santa in his mid-fifties. He sports a large beer belly and an expression of continual disgust. SANTA TWO is an aging wino. His back is to the audience, as he tries to sleep off his latest binge on a bed of old newspapers. SANTA THREE is a young woman in her late twenties, with no beard, but a perpetually angry expression. SANTA FOUR is a stoned slacker, with his real beard extending below his white wig and Santa cap, instead of a fake one. He sits cross-legged by the Stage Left wall. Santa Five looks at the others with stunned disbelief.)

FIVE. I don't believe it...

TWO. *(Rolling over.)* Awww, crap. Not another one!

THREE. Okay. As long as you are here, I'll warn you exactly like I warned the others. There are boundaries and personal space issues that need to be respected. Just because we're locked in here and we are all Santas does not mean we have a single thing in common. Or grants you permission to interact with me in any manner whatsoever!

FIVE. This can't be happening...

FOUR. Oh, but it is, dude. Swallow the red velvet pill and journey down the rabbit hole. Enjoy the now. Even if this particular trip is a Santa-filled hostage situation.

ONE. Ignore the psychobabble from squidbrain over there. He thinks he's one of them neo-retro-stoner-slacker types. He talks about living in the now, but his brain is set on half-past Woodstock.

FOUR. The 1960's were a righteously beautiful time, old dude.

ONE. How the hell would you know? You weren't even a date rape fantasy in your granddaddy's eye until the '90s.

FOUR. That's enslavement to calendar talk, old dude. Don't you know virtual reality is like virtually real, and like a wormhole through space-time?

ONE. Never knew anyone who could make internet trolls sound sane by comparison. Uh, where was I?

FOUR. Welcome committee, man.

ONE. Did I ask you?! *(To Five.)* Okay, to keep things straight, you are Santa Five.

FIVE. Santa Five?

ONE. Yeah. Names aren't exactly a priority here. It's not like any of us ever want to connect again after this thing is over.

FOUR. Welcome to the machine.

ONE. I'd like to welcome your head to the sweet spot on my nine iron.

FOUR. Negativity, man. Bad karma. I coulda been eating laced brownies and binge-watching video game championships on the Geek Channel. Instead, I get shoved in a cellar with Klu Klux Santa.

ONE. Ignore the wastoid. Anyway, we're going by the order that the fruitcake nabbed us. I'm Santa One. *(Gestures to the Wino on the floor.)* This raggedy thing that smells like the morning after a bachelor party is Santa Two.

TWO. Keep it down...I'm shleepin' here.

ONE. *(Points to the woman.)* Santa Three... Although I can't imagine why any guy...even a psycho...would want to grab her.

THREE. Have I told you to eat excrement lately? *(Turns to Five.)* Remember, this state takes sexual harassment very seriously. No Hashtag MeToo moments, or Stockholm syndrome foreplay allowed. You come on to me, and I'll make sure pieces of you start coming off you. I don't care if it 'tis the season to be jolly.' You ain't getting your jollies with me!

FIVE. Uh... charmed, I'm sure.

ONE. Don't expect to see that one on the cover of a Victoria Secret catalogue any time soon... *(Points to Four.)* Last...and definitely least...the poster child for the "I No Longer Fit In This Universe" Campaign... Your freak and mine... Santa Four.

FOUR. Merry Christmas. This is sorta like our own Santapallooza...only without all the sex, drugs and rock and roll. Still, might as well make the best of it. Since he snatched us on Christmas Eve, the odds are, he's not a religious fanatic. So probability of being beheaded on video is low.

FIVE. Comforting.

FOUR. *(Smiles.)* Gotta stoke the silver lining.

FIVE. How long have you all been here?

ONE. I've been cooped up with this fruit and nut brigade about six hours.

FIVE. Have you tried figuring a way out?

(They all look at each other. Pause, then…)

FIVE. Okay. That was probably a stupid question.

ONE. What the hell you think we've been doing down here? Jingling our bells? We tried everything short of having that hashhead gnaw through the steel door.

FIVE. No windows?

ONE. No windows. No air vents. Not even a mousehole. That's the only door and it's too thick to break down. The psycho knew what he was doing. That sicko son of a…

THREE. Hey! We can do without that kind of language.

ONE. Do my big bad words hurt your virgin ears?

THREE. Eat shit and die.

TWO. What the hell? Can't a Santa get any sleep around here?

THREE. You too, Two!

TWO. *(Rolls back over.)* Well, pardon me for breathing! *(Burps.)*

THREE. That's not breathing. That's polluting.

FOUR. Negativity, man. I warned you.

ONE. As I was saying before I was so rudely interrupted…

THREE. Ha!

ONE. …was that the whacko started his crime spree about six hours ago. He seems to grab another Santa every hour and sixteen minutes.

FIVE. You time him?

ONE. There ain't a hell of a lot else to do around here. The company ain't exactly what you'd consider 'prime cut.' Unless you like talking to a wino, a wierdo and a lesbian.

THREE. I am not a lesbian! Not that there's anything wrong with that…

ONE. You go to college in Massachusetts?

THREE. How did you know?

ONE. You vote Democrat?

THREE. Of course.

ONE. Then you're a lesbian.

THREE. Exactly the type of caveman logic I'd expect from a troglodyte like you.

ONE. If you ain't a lesbian, how come you're a Santa?

THREE. It's a free country last time I checked! And who said mythical characters can't be gender-fluid?

ONE. Why couldn't you just be Mrs. Claus? Not butch enough for ya?

THREE. Watch it, One… or you're gonna be missing your sack of toys!

ONE. Real lady-like, wouldn't you say. Five?

FIVE. I'd rather not get in the middle of…

THREE. Yeah, what is your opinion, Santa Five?

ONE. Go ahead. Tell us what you think of our little Saint Dyke?

THREE. Well?!

FIVE. Uh… I guess… I mean, um…couldn't you have been an elf or something, maybe?

THREE. Aaaaaaarrrrgggh! Men!

FIVE. I'm sorry. I didn't mean to…

THREE. You are all alike! Tunnel-visioned, knuckle-dragging Harvey Weinsteins!

FIVE. I'm sorry. I'm just not used to female Santas.

THREE. Like there's some kind of glass ceiling up at the North Pole? Aren't there any sensitive men left in the world? Can't any of them understand how a woman really feels?

FOUR. I understand what you're feeling.

THREE. Shut up, moron. I'm being rhetorical!

FOUR. Harsh. Way harsh.

THREE. Your entire patriarchal plutocracy is so damned insensitive...

FIVE. Really, I'm sorry. I didn't know it meant so much to you.

THREE. Don't patronize me. I already have a father!

ONE. Yeah? What's her name?

THREE. Bite me.

ONE. I'm afraid my teeth would break.

FIVE. Why don't you ease up? Can't you see she's upset?

ONE. Great. Another bleeding heart liberal! And I thought the freak-osopher and the lipstick lesbian were bad enough.

FOUR. You become what you resist.

ONE. Yeah? Well, I'd like to resist a baseball bat, so's I could knock some sense into your furry little head!

FIVE. Why don't we all calm down? This is hardly the time for hostilities.

THREE. New guy's right...even if he does sound like such a wussy boy.

FIVE. What?

ONE. He's not a wussy boy. He's a wimp. We got us a wino, a weirdo, a dyke and a wimp!

THREE. I'm not a dyke!

ONE. *(Shrugs.)* Can't prove it by me.

FIVE. Cut it out, One! It's bad enough we all have to be here. We don't need a bellyaching Santa pushing us at each other's throats.

FOUR. I hear you. I know where you're coming from.

FIVE.   You stay out of this, Four.

FOUR.   More negativity. Damn.

>   *(In frustration, One throws himself against the door, but the door doesn't budge. He rubs his sore shoulder and sits on the floor.)*

ONE.   I'm in Holiday Hell... Hey, wino. Pass the bottle.

TWO.   Grab your own. They're over there.

>   *(One rifles through some boxes and pulls out a few bottles of wine.)*

FIVE.   Could you throw me one, One?

>   *(One grumbles and tosses him a bottle. Five examines the label.)*

FIVE.   Thanks. Hmmm. Chateau St. Emillion. It seems our captor has pretty sophisticated taste.

ONE.   You're not going all Stockholm Syndrome on us now, are you?

FIVE.   No. All I meant was that this is a fairly expensive French Burgundy. And a very good vintage.

TWO.   My thoughts exactly. *(Buuuuurp.)*

FIVE.   My point was, your average punk would have picked a cheaper wine. This guy plans things. Pays attention to details. That tells us something about him. We may be able to use that to our advantage.

ONE.   Well, aren't we Mister 'CSI – North Pole?'

FIVE.   I pride myself on being a student of human behavior. You can tell a lot about a person by what they drink.

TWO.   I concur.

ONE.   Thanks for the advice, Professor Wussyboy. You give me a nine-millimeter automatic and I'll invite our host over for a special wine tasting. *(Pantomimes a wine glass.)* A fine bouquet. A robust flavor. A slight aftertaste of lead. *(Pantomimes shooting him.)* Bam. Bam. Bam. Bam!

FIVE.   You've watched your share of Rambo movies, haven't you?

ONE.   Yeah. What of it?

FIVE. Nothing. Nothing.

FOUR. How do you know so much about human behavior, Five?

FIVE. I'm a licensed marriage counselor.

THREE. Really? How long have you been married?

FIVE. I'm not married.

THREE. Divorced?

FIVE. No.

THREE. Separated?

FIVE. Actually, I've never been married.

ONE. So I guess knowing what the hell you're talking about isn't one of the job qualifications in your line of work?

FIVE. There's no need for sarcasm.

ONE. No need for orgasms either. But they sure are fun.

THREE. So based on your total lack of anything related to marital experience, you believe yourself capable of telling other people how they should feel and behave? What is it about testosterone that makes all men think they're automatically a cross between Albert Einstein and God?

FIVE. Direct experience doesn't always equate to knowledge and insight.

ONE. Maybe. But when I was a combat pilot in the Air Force, it made me feel just a tiny bit better knowing the guy teaching me to fly had been up in a plane at least once in his life.

FIVE. Maybe it's just that I haven't found the right woman.

ONE. That's what the farmer said to his sheep, every time he took the flock out on a Saturday night.

FIVE. Why do you always have to make jokes at other people's expense?

ONE. I'm not sure. But my anger management class told me it was wonderful therapy.

(Five turns to Four in exasperation.)

FOUR. Don't look at me, man. I think marriage is an archaic institution. Nothing more than state-licensed sex by contract.

FIVE. You've been dumped, haven't you.

FOUR. Thirty-two times. The pawn shop is getting tired of me hocking the same engagement ring.

FIVE. I always tell my clients you can't give up on love because of a few bad experiences.

ONE. They're dumb enough to pay to hear that. I can ignore you for free.

(Santa One turns and sulks in the corner. Santa Two has passed out again, and Santa Four is rocking out to the music in his head. Five turns to Santa Three in desperation.)

FIVE. So... you come here often? (Shrinks from her angry expression.) It's a joke. A little humor to lighten the mood.

THREE. I find it hard to be amused by your poorly disguised animosity towards women.

FIVE. Animosity?

THREE. Disgust. Jealousy. Contempt. When you feel threatened or uncomfortable, you turn to the only woman in the place and diminish her with a patronizing pick-up line. Was I supposed to blush and bat my eyelashes and wait for you to rescue helpless little me from this situation? Because as far as I can see, that door is still locked and you're still a pig.

TWO. You tell him, sishter!

THREE. Aren't you late for your diabetic coma?

FIVE. I'm sorry. It was just a joke.

THREE. There's no such thing as 'just a joke.' It's nothing more than brutality with a smile. Why do you think they call it a 'punchline?'

ONE. *(Laughing.)* Better not take her to a comedy club on your first date.

FIVE. I was only trying to lighten the tension, that's all.

THREE. Don't try that old 'It'll-release-all-your-tension, baby' line with me, Mister Relationship Expert. I've been down that mattress before. Oh, you may think you're all so evolved, but as far as I can see, you're all just three footstomps out of the cave and still obsessing about the size of your club!

ONE. She got you there, wimp-boy.

FIVE. Really, I didn't mean anything by it.

THREE. Of course not! Don't ever let even the remotest possibility of meaningful conversation creep into your sexual harassment.

FIVE. What sexual harassment? Look, I'm sorry if I offended you.

THREE. Why are you so hostile towards us? What did our entire gender ever do to you?

ONE. Not much...by the look of him.

FIVE. What's that supposed to mean?

ONE. Hey, if the ruby slipper fits...

FIVE. Oh, because I refuse to abuse or condescend to women, you automatically assume I'm gay?

ONE. *(Shrugs.)* That'd explain why you hang out with elves..

FOUR. It's nothing to be ashamed of, Five. I think being a gay marriage counselor takes real courage. Besides, it's legal in a few countries now.

FIVE. I'm not gay!

ONE. Come out of the closet or stay in it. It's your lifestyle.

FIVE. Nobody's coming out of the closet! I wasn't in the closet to begin with! Uh...not that there's anything wrong with it...

THREE. Spoken like a real politically correct hatemonger.

FIVE. I have lots of friends who are gay. Seven! Well, six and a half, because technically Randy goes both ways...

ONE. And how many ways do you go, kid?

THREE. Leave pansy boy alone, One! He has enough problems with his all-consuming hatred of women.

FIVE. I'm not a pansy boy! And I don't hate women!

ONE. That's right. He's not a pansy boy.

FIVE. That's right.

ONE. He's a wussy boy. That's what she called him.

FIVE. So now you're listening to her?

ONE. Hey, don't blame me for your confused sexual idenity.

FOUR. Not that there's anything wrong with that.

FIVE. I do not have a confused sexual identity! And even if I did, I sure wouldn't accept your diagnosis of me…or hers!

THREE. I suppose you didn't mean anything by that comment either?

FIVE. Well, no…I didn't. Or maybe I did…I'm sorry. That was uncalled for.

THREE. Standard operating procedures for those with Y chromosomes.

ONE. Which may or may not apply to him.

FIVE. Shut up, One!

FOUR. It's okay, Five. I happen to like Lady Gaga and the Fashion Channel.

FIVE. Will you all stop picking on me?!

ONE. Sounds a bit paranoid to me. Don't let us interrupt your mental melt-down.

FIVE. *(Jumping up.)* I'm not having a mental melt-down! I am constructively voicing my frustration in a positive… *(Suddenly embarrassed.)* …and overly loud…uh, voice…

(Five sits. Embarrassed. An awkward silence.)

THREE. So people actually pay you to help them solve their emotional problems?

ONE. Well…I know I feel purged…

FIVE. I'm not operating at my peak here. In case you haven't noticed, I've been under a bit of stress with this whole kidnapping thing.

ONE. Look at that. He can't even take responsibility for getting pissed. What a wuss…

FIVE. Aaaaaaarrrrrggh!

(Five leaps up and throws himself ferociously at the larger man. Santa One simply raises his hand, which connects with Five's forehead, knocking him backward on his butt.)

ONE. By the way, wussy boy. You fight like a girl. You really should get your mama to give you some boxing lessons.

(Santa Three casually gets up and saunters over to the big man.)

ONE. And what do you want, little girl?

THREE. Haaayyaaaah!!

(She throws a single punch to the belly, knocking him to the floor.)

THREE. My mama was a third-degree black belt. She fought like a girl too.

FOUR. Awesome! I am so gonna pick you as my avatar in my next video game.

(Santa Three sits back down and opens a small bottle of pills. Every few minutes, she pops another one in her mouth.)

FIVE. Uh, Thanks for taking my side.

THREE. I wasn't. He had it coming.

FIVE. I guess there are times karate can be as effective as counseling.

THREE. Is that your professional opinion?

FIVE. In his case…you bet.

THREE. You're not a very good counselor, are you?

FIVE. No, I'm not. Evidently, I'm just a pretentious ass who can pontificate about other people's problems but can't even identify his own.

THREE. Sounds like a pretty accurate diagnosis to me.

FIVE.   I can't believe I let that guy get to me like that.

FOUR.   Guys like that specialize in getting to people. *(Indicating Three.)* And people like her always believe they're being gotten.

THREE.   You two are talking about me, aren't you?

FOUR.   What makes you think we're talking about you?

THREE.   Your nostrils are flaring.

FOUR.   *(Touches his nose.)* Are they? Cool...

THREE.   It's a primitive male instinct going all the way back to Neanderthal days. Men do that right before they are going to attack something...or someone.

FIVE.   Nobody is going to attack you, Three. We're on your side.

THREE.   Yeah. That's what Sitting Bull said to General Custer. That's what the Hitler said to Stalin. That's what pimply-faced Leonard Witherspoon said to me in the back seat of his VW bug.

FOUR.   Been there. Done that. Demands extreme flexibility.

THREE.   You can't help yourselves. All men are predators and they consider all women their prey. And I'm so damned tired of being used...

FIVE.   Don't you think that sounds a tiny bit paranoid?

THREE.   Don't talk to me about paranoia. Talk to them!

FIVE.   Them? Them who?

THREE.   Let me remind you that 'Paranoia' is a term coined by psychologists - male psychologists - to keep us in our place.

ONE.   Here we go again.

THREE.   Why do you hate us so much? Why must you vent your hostilities and sick repressions on those who are most willing to nurture you?

TWO.   Third time tonight I heard this speech...

FIVE.   I...I don't try to. I really do respect women.

ONE.   Don't let her bully you, kid. Act like a man!

THREE. And do what? Smack me around?

ONE. Only until your tongue stops tap dancing.

THREE. *(Rising.)* That does it! This time, you're going down for good!!

(Three leaps at One, but Four and Five hold her back.)

FIVE. Grab her, Four. Hold her back!

(No matter how hard she struggles, they will not let her go.)

THREE. It's a conspiracy! You're all in this together!

FOUR. Easy, sister. Chill a bit. I spent most of my life listening to jerks like him. You can't let them get to you. He only wants to push your buttons.

FIVE. Four is right. You can get him madder by just smiling and ignoring what he says. Act cool.

ONE. You can't cool down someone who's frigid.

THREE. Frigid! Frigid?! I'll have you know I melted better men than you!

ONE. Yeah. But most of them were inflatable.

FIVE. One!!

THREE. I'll kill him!

(She lunges again but is still restrained by Four and Five. The pills have started to make her woozy and unsteady on her feet.)

FIVE. Calm down, Three!!

THREE. *(Crumples.)* I hate you all. I hate your arrogance. I hate your condescension. I hate your hormones!

ONE. Guess who ain't getting my vote for Miss Congeniality.

FIVE. Stuff it in your stocking, Santa! *(To Three.)* Calm down, Three. We're not all...

THREE. Just leave me alone! All of you! Just leave me alone!

(She pulls away from the others and retreats to a corner, Stage Left. She pulls out a second bottle of pills, continues swallowing them throughout the following. Her movements are getting slower, more erratic.)

THREE.   What time is it, anyway?

FOUR.   A little after eleven, I think. Coming up on midnight, Christmas Eve.

ONE.   What difference does it make? We're all gonna rot in here.

THREE.   Who asked you?

ONE.   Lady, you are a guaranteed cure for a Viagra overdose.

THREE.   And you could be the advertising campaign for 'America's Got Morons."

ONE.   Moron? I happen to be a hardhat and a Gulf War veteran! I was dodging shrapnel while you were safe at home crying over Sex & The City reruns!!

FIVE.   Excuse me, but aren't you taking an awful lot of those pills?

THREE.   What's it to you? You a pharmaceutical counselor now?

FIVE.   I only meant I don't think it's a good idea to take so many.

THREE.   Mind your own business. This is something I've been planning to do for a long time. Seven and a half months...

(He snatches the bottle from her, looks at the label.)

FIVE.   Are you crazy? This stuff will kill you!

THREE.   Give me back my pills!

FIVE.   No! You are going to kill yourself if you take that many.

THREE.   Give me back my pills!

FIVE.   No!

THREE.   Please? Haven't you done enough to me already?

FIVE.   I am not going to sit here and let you kill yourself!

ONE.   Great. I can see the headlines now... 'Hostage dyke turns suicidal Santa.'

THREE. What do you know about my life? You think your little marriage counseling certificate tells you anything about what it's like to be me?!

FIVE. No, it doesn't... But it does help me recognize pain when I see it.

(She is much weaker now. Flails blindly at the bottle in his hand.)

THREE. Give me back...my pills...

FIVE. I don't care what hardships or heartaches you've had in life. Nothing can be this bad.

THREE. Oh, yes it can... You have no idea...

FIVE. Please, let me help you.

THREE. I don't want your help. I don't need your help... I'm not your patient... give me back those pills...

FIVE. I can't let you hurt yourself.

THREE. ...'s my choice... I don't belong in a world that values pectorals over...personality. Where IQs get less use than IUDs...

FIVE. A few bad attitudes are not worth dying over.

THREE. ...where no one cares at all, unless you look like the Playmate of the Month...

FIVE. You're wrong...

THREE. *(Struggling to her feet.)* Don't you dare tell me I'm wrong! All my life... ever since I was a little girl... you men have trapped me behind walls of inferiority... ever since I can remember, you smothered me with pink dresses, Barbie dolls and tea party manners... they all tell me what I can do and what I can't... what I can be and what I can't...And if I ever dared to do what I wanted to do...I'd be shouted down with horrified stares...or stupid insults from men like him...

(She waves a weak arm in One's direction. She is really getting disoriented now.)

THREE. Well, newsflash, mister, you man you... I hate the color pink...and this...this is one thing I can do to prove you all can't use me anymore! Now gimme that bottle!

(Three leaps at Five who clutches the bottle. He tries to fight her off, even though she pummels him.)

FIVE. No! Suicide never solved anything!

FOUR. Actually, if you read Sartre, he would disagree...

FIVE. Shut up, Four! One, give me a hand here. *(Grabs her flailing arm.)* Stop fighting, Three!

THREE. Ow! You're hurting me. *(Weakly.)* Can't everyone stop hurting me...?

(She collapses to the floor. The pills are really taking effect now, and she finds it difficult to sit up.)

FIVE. I will. Once you promise to forget about killing yourself.

THREE. Why don't you just rape me and make my humiliation complete?

FIVE. I don't want to rape you.

THREE. Oh, I'm not good looking enough for you? Is that it?

FIVE. That's not it at all. I think you are sweet and smart and amazingly attractive.

(She is fading fast. Her voice reverts to that of a small child.)

THREE. You're just saying that to keep me from vomiting on you...

FIVE. No...well, yes. But I also want you to live.

THREE. ... why?

FIVE. Why? Because... because you should.

FOUR. He's right.

THREE. ...another 'should'...

FIVE. I don't want you to die.

THREE. ... why...?

FIVE. Because I would feel bad.

THREE. ...you would?

FIVE. Of course.

FOUR. We all would.

THREE. ...really...?

FIVE. Men can show compassion too, you know.

THREE. ...oh... *(Barely holding her head up.)* ...are you a transvestite...?

ONE. Ha!

FIVE. Why are you being so cynical?

(She rallies a bit. She sits up, but her speech becomes distorted and slurred.)

THREE. ...cynical...cynical is all they leave you... all they ever leave you... When you're good...and work hard...but they pay someone more... just because they can...I don't know...grow a beard...Cynical is when your boss... expects favors... that leave you feeling cheap...and dirty... Cynical is when... when your boyfriend runs off with your step-mom...

FOUR. Your step-mom?

THREE. ...and your car...and all your savings... all that leaves you is cynical...

FIVE. I'm so sorry.

THREE. ... don't be sorry... Don't you dare feel sorry for me... I'm a big girl... a woman... I can take care of myself...

FIVE. Of course you can.

THREE. *(Distantly.)* ...she had bigger boobs; you know... the tramp he left my mom for musta had forty-eight double D's... Maybe double G's... or W's. Do they go all the way to W's?

FIVE. That's just the pills talking.

THREE. *(Eyes going wide.)* The pills can talk?!

(She picks up the empty bottle to apologize to it.)

THREE. *(To the bottle.)* I'm so sorry…. I didn't know you could talk! I just thought you were…you know…pills… *(To Five.)* … I feel kinda funny… do you know anyone with forty-eight double W's..? ..real ones, I mean..?

FIVE. No. It doesn't matter. All that matters is that we get you feeling better, okay?

THREE. … mine are thirty-threes, you know… 'B' cups… most men, that's all they notice about you…

FIVE. Not me. The first thing I noticed was your eyes.

THREE. …my eyes..?

FIVE. They are really beautiful. Grey, with just the slightest specks of green. Oh, and your Santa costume. I noticed that too.

THREE. …you noticed my eyes? I have two of them you know…

FIVE. I know. How about you and me try to walk off those pills. And then maybe we can talk more, okay?

THREE. With the pills? They can talk you know… I wish someone had told me that earlier…Hate to think of them having a conversation in my stomach … *(Giggles drunkenly.)* Hey…it's dark in here! Oh yeah, just wait 'til we get to her intestines! Hee hee hee…

FIVE. That's the best 'talking pill' impression I ever heard. But try to focus… How many of these pills did you take?

THREE. I don't know… maybe forty or fifty…

FIVE. Forty or fifty?! We have to get you to vomit!

(Five tries to pick Three up as she is too weak to stand.)

ONE. Vomit? That's disgusting.

TWO. Wha..? Did I do it again?

(Two feels the floor around him and finds nothing. He rolls over on his side again.)

FIVE. Give me a hand with her, Four! *(To Three.)* It'll be okay. You are going to be all right.

THREE. ...this is really very nice of you... most men aren't this nice...unless you got big boobs...

FIVE. I'm not most men.

FOUR. She's going to be okay. Isn't she?

FIVE. *(Frightened.)* I don't know...

THREE. ... I... I'm sorry I called you a wussy boy... you're not really a wussy boy, you know...

FIVE. I know. Just please don't die on me...

(Five ad Four drag her off, Stage Right. One looks through the curtain at them, then paces the stage. He is clearly concerned but doesn't know what to do... and that's a feeling he can't stand. After a moment, a strange look crosses his face. He turns to the sleeping wino.)

ONE. Did you just..?

TWO. *(Without turning over.)* It happens.

ONE. Great... We've got a suicidal Santa with her head in a bucket... and I'm left alone with the Ghost of Christmas Gas!

CURTAIN

End of Act One

ACT TWO

AT RISE. Later that evening. Santa Two is still passed out on the floor. Empty wine bottles everywhere. Santa One, having drank a bit too much himself, has assembled a circle of half mannequins around him, and is playing 'Spin The Bottle' with them.)

ONE. Okay, Esmerelda. It's your turn to Spin The Bottle. What's that? You want me to spin for you? Well, if you insist...

(He gives the empty bottle a spin.)

ONE. How about that? It's you and me again!

(He looks around to make sure no one is watching, then picks up the half a mannequin and gives it a quick kiss.)

TWO. And I thought the guy who kidnapped us was bonkers...

ONE. How long have you been awake?

TWO. *(Without turning over.)* Long enough to be glad I'm not a mannequin.

(Santa One starts to pace again.)

ONE. I don't know how much longer I can take this!

(The steel door flies open. One jumps back as a young Santa is pushed onstage.)

BERNIE. *(Offstage.)* Get in there, elf-boy!

(SANTA SIX is thin, Hispanic, with no beard and no belly. His Santa costume is more like a tight and shiny red suit, with more stylish boots. One looks on dubiously, as Santa Six yells at the steel door.)

SIX. If I ever get a hold of your sister, man!

ONE. *(Shaking his head.)* Wonderful. Just wonderful.

SIX. Who are you?

ONE. Who do I look like?

SIX. Santa Claus.

ONE. Bright boy. I never heard of a spic Santa before.

SIX. Watchu say?!

ONE. Nothing personal. But you can't tell me anybody really believes you are the real Saint Nick. I mean, look at you... you got no beard. No belly... And you ain't never gonna get a tan like that at the North Pole.

SIX. You got yourself a problem, man?

ONE. *(Sighs.)* I hate to see Christmas go ethnic.

SIX. I only got one thing to say to you.

ONE. Yeah? What's that?

SIX. Santa Claus.

ONE. Huh?

SIX. Santa Claus. Santa Claus...

ONE. So?

SIX. So you telling me that 'Santa Claus' sounds Caucasian?

ONE. *(Mouths it to himself.)* You got a point there.

SIX. Let me tell you. The man's a home boy. And you see his sled, man? I mean, he's the original low rider.

ONE. That explains why there's no hubcaps on his reindeer.

SIX. Your mama.

ONE. What about her?

TWO. Keep it down, will ya?

SIX. Who's he? No, don't tell me...

ONE & SIX. *(Together.)* Santa Claus...

ONE. And notice he's not bilingual.

SIX. Looks like he has enough problems with only one tongue.

ONE. Yeah. Look, I don't mean to come down hard on you or anything, but don't you feel like a clown in that get-up?

SIX. You telling me you don't feel like a clown in yours?

(One looks at his Santa suit, then smiles. Hands Six a wine bottle.)

ONE. Aw, what the heck. Have some wine, kid.

SIX. *(Sitting beside him.)* Gracias. I don't normally imbibe with brain-dead racists... but I guess you don't normally drink with any of us pigmentally challenged types either.

ONE. Not in public.

SIX. Maybe you should. Then you wouldn't be so scared of us.

ONE. You think I'm scared of you?

SIX. In my neighborhood, you stay healthy by knowing who is scared of you and who ain't. So maybe the man has a little twitch or shake in his voice or something... But you pick it up, and he knows you pick it up... and you stay healthy. You? You're just scared of anything that don't look exactly like you.

ONE. What the hell do you know? You're just a punk kid.

SIX. Yeah. I'm a punk kid and you're a phony old redneck tryin' to be the meanest dude in town... But it's okay. I'll try to be scared of you if you want. *(Lifts his bottle.)* To all the white folk who first settled America.

ONE. Now you're talking.

(They clink bottles and toast.)

SIX. ... who couldn't have found there way here if it wasn't for a crazy wop sailor and the Spanish queen who picked up the tab for his ride.

ONE. You tryin' to tell me that Columbus would never have discovered America without the Spaniards?

SIX. Hey, if the ship fits, sail it.

ONE. And how many of you wetbacks signed the Declaration of Independence?

SIX.   None. We had better things to do than fight a war that starts with a tea party. And no ancestor of mine would be caught dead in those poofy powdered wigs they wore. They'd be laughed out of the barrio.

ONE.   Yeah? Well, we kicked your butts big-time in the Mexican American War.

SIX.   Naw, man. After the Alamo, we just lost interest... And we never wanted Texas anyway. Too many Texans, you hear what I'm saying?

ONE.   *(Smiles.)* You know something, kid? You're all right. Cheers..

SIX.   Salute`.

(They toast. Santa Three enters through the Stage Right curtain, aided by Santas Five and Four.)

THREE.   Really. I'm fine now.

FIVE.   *(Noticing Six.)* Who's he?

ONE, TWO & SIX.   Santa Claus.

FOUR.   Hmm. Good harmony.

ONE.   You feeling better?

THREE.   What did you say?

ONE.   Just wanted to make sure you weren't gonna up and die on us or anything. No big deal.

THREE.   I'm okay... Thanks for asking.

ONE.   Like I said. No big deal. This here is Santa Six.

SIX.   Santa Six?

ONE.   It's better than one of those three-mile-long Mexican names. Like Don Rodrigo Gonzalez Burrito, or something.

SIX.   Do they ever come and take shavings of your brain for fertilizer samples?

ONE.   Hey, I'm in charge of the insults around here.

SIX.   Yeah, then who explains them to you?

ONE. Your mama.

> *(They both smile and give each other a 'high five.')*

SIX. I'll make a redneck of you yet.

ONE. Only if I get a lobotomy first.

> *(They slap another 'high five.')*

SIX. Good one!

FOUR. Why do I feel like we just stepped into the Twilight Zone?

ONE. Don't mind the slack-jawed loser. He's Santa Four. That's Santa Five. The Wino's Two and I'm Santa One.

FOUR. Don't forget Santa Three.

ONE. Like I could.

SIX. Buenos Dias. You feelin' sick, Santa lady?

THREE. It's nothing... A little case of attempted suicide brought on by seven months of depression over what I thought was typical male aggression.

FIVE. Ahem...

THREE. But these Santas showed me that I might have over-generalized a bit..

TWO. *(Rolling over.)* Huh? You mean she didn't die?

THREE. Not tonight. *(Smiles up at Five.)* Let's say I put those pill plans on hold for a while.

FIVE. A long while, I hope.

THREE. There's still nothing in it for you, you realize.

FIVE. I think you've made that abundantly clear. Besides, the image of you spewing your intestines into that steel bucket is not exactly something that inspires romance. *(Happily.)* And since none of us can seem to get out of here, we might as well make the most of it. Whatta you say?

FOUR. That's the spirit! How 'bout we sing *Heck The Dolls* or *Violent Kites* and all those other Christmassy Classics?

SIX. That dude been smoking kitty litter?

ONE. Naw. That's just what happens when cousins marry.

FOUR. *(Singing.)*
OH, THERE'S NO SPACE LIKE HOSTAGE FOR THE HOLIDAYS.

SIX. Bing Crosby, he ain't.

ONE. You know Bing Crosby?

SIX. Sure. White Christmas. Typical racist song. But the man had good pipes.

ONE. Amigo, you surprise me.

SIX. No problem, man. You all know *Jingle Bells?* Heh? *(Singing.)*
DASHING THROUGH THE SNOW...

FOUR & SIX. *(Singing.)*
IN A ONE HORSE OPEN SLEIGH...

SIX. *(To One.)* C'mon, Amigo. Show us whatchu got.

ONE, FOUR, FIVE & SIX. *(Singing.)*
O'ER THE FIELDS WE GO...

ALL. *(Singing.)*
LAUGHING ALL THE WAY!

TWO.
Ha ha ha!

ONE, FOUR, FIVE & SIX. *(Singing.)*
BELLS ON BOB TAILS RING...

FOUR. Hold it.

ONE, FIVE & SIX. *(Singing.)*
MAKING SPIRITS BRIGHT...

FOUR. Wait a second...

(The song grinds to a stop, as everyone looks at Santa Four.)

ONE. What now?

FOUR. What are bob tails?

FIVE. I don't know.

SIX. Me, neither.

FIVE. Aren't they the tails on horses?

FOUR. I thought horses had long tails?

ONE. Dammit all! The squidbrain spoiled our song!

FOUR. I only wanted to know. I've been singing it for years and I never knew what it meant.

ONE. Bob tails are horse tails, you moron!

FOUR. But horses have long tails?

ONE. So they cut them off for the song! And for that you had to spoil the whole damn mood!

SIX. Chill, old dude. We can sing more. We got time.

FIVE. Yeah... we got time.

FOUR. Time is all we got.

FIVE. Maybe months.

ONE. Or worse... Hours.

(They all stop and silently consider the situation they're in... and the bleaker prospects which may await them. One and Six chug heavily from their bottles.)

FIVE. Hey. does anyone know how long until midnight?

TWO. Eleven minutes, twenty-one seconds.

ONE. Wonderful. We got us a digital wino.

TWO. Eight thousand, six hundred and fifty-one minutes to New Year's.

ONE. Yeah, right. And how many seconds?

(Two sits up and thinks for a moment.)

TWO. Five hundred and eighteen thousand, four hundred and thirty-nine.

FIVE. Wow. How'd you do that?

TWO. I'm... *(Burp.)* ...good with numbers.

ONE. Like eighty-six proof.

TWO. Go on. Ask me anything.

FIVE. Okay. What's one hundred and ninety-four times four thousand and seven?

TWO. Seven hundred and seventy-seven thousand, three hundred and fifty eight.

FIVE. Divided by eighteen?

TWO. Forty-three thousand, one hundred and eighty-six, point five, five, five, five six... Rounded up of course.

FIVE. That's incredible.

FOUR. Ninety-seven times four?

TWO. Three hundred eighty-eight.

FIVE. One hundred eighty-four million divided by twenty-six point two?

TWO. Uh, let's see... carry the nine... *(Smiles.)* Seven million, twenty-two thousand, nine hundred and seven!

FOUR. Awesome!

TWO. Yup.

FIVE. Not that I mean to knock your lifestyle choices, but you really should have done something with that talent of yours.

TWO. I did do something. The booze helps me undo it.

ONE. Don't tell me he's one of those "I drink to forget winos"...

FOUR. Give him a chance, man.

TWO. Wassa matter? You think just because I'm a drunk by profession, I ain't got no brain cells?

ONE. None that aren't fermenting.

TWO. There was a time I could have bought and sold any of you... I was one of the best corporate accountants this city ever saw!

ONE. Do we have to listen to this?

SIX. Chill out, amigo. I want to hear the old dude's story.

FOUR. In vino veritas.

TWO. That's the truth. There's more geniuses on Skid Row than in half the elected offices in this country!

SIX. There are more politicians on Skid Row than in half the elected offices in this country.

FIVE. So what happened to you?

TWO. It was so long ago... *(Slips back into the memory.)* I used to be a top CPA... Number sixty-two in one of the Big Eight accounting firms... Senior Partner... plush office, plush house, plush secretary...

(He stops to take a long swallow from the bottle he grips tightly.)

TWO. It ain't as easy as you think. I had to fight my way to the top... clawing through endless boxes of little numbers, climbing over the bodies of those poor bastards addicted to calculators and adding machines... Yeah, you people don't realize it, but accountancy is played for keeps!

ONE. Ain't that a load of...

THREE & FOUR. Ssssh!

FIVE. So what happened? Couldn't you take the pressure?

TWO. Pressure? Hell. I could take anything they threw at me. Back then, I was a master of the game. I had the killer instinct. It got so's I could look a man in the eye and tell right then and there whether or not his books were balanced...

(His voice grows stronger. And he swaggers with a gleam in his eye.)

TWO. I could reduce the most powerful corporate executive to a quivering mass of Cool Whip just by shaking my head and going. "Tsk, tsk, tsk"...

ONE. You know, I think I liked him better passed out.

TWO. The pen may be mightier than the sword, but in my hand, the number two lead was a strategic weapon... But you can't rest on your laurels in an accounting firm. One day, Numbers 63, 72 and 91 tried to move up on me. Wanted to put another notch on their Cross pens. They'd been watching me for days, observing my every debit, checking spreadsheets when my back was turned... just waiting for their chance... Then, that afternoon...at exactly high noon, they called me out in front of the whole firm. They whipped out an early ledger of mine and pointed it at me, saying they found some... improprieties.... I looked around for back-up from my co-workers. My partners. But they were scared... Rabbits, all of them. They suggested I resign quietly. Leave the company. Take the easy way out.... But I couldn't do that. Sometimes, a man has got to stand up and be an accountant...no matter what the risk...

ONE. Is this guy for real?

THREE, FOUR, FIVE & SIX. Sssshhh!

TWO. So I faced them alone... They reached for their calculators, but I was quicker. I remembered the Freeman Effect for relativistic monetary theory. It was a desperate gamble, but it worked. None of them knew it's fundamentals. I plugged in the equations before they could even draw their own conclusions.

(Two spins the tale like he's on fire. The others are mesmerized.)

TWO. *(Grimly.)* They didn't stand a chance. Humiliated in the eyes of senior management. When the smoke cleared, I had knocked them back to 84, 112 and 214...respectively.

FOUR. So, you won?

(Two takes another swig of wine and grimaces.)

TWO. Yeah, I won.. But it was a bloody business. The dazed look in their eyes was pitiful to see. Their careers were in tatters, their credibility gone.
MORE

TWO. *(Continued.)* And an accountant without his credibility is like a hooker with a plutonium chastity belt. Ain't nobody gonna want your services anymore... *(Swallows hard.)* Anyway, that's when things started to go bad. Call it guilt, maybe, but the figures started to follow me home...

FIVE. The figures?

TWO. Everywhere I'd go, I'd see little penciled-in numbers. They were always around, multiplying faster than I could add them up.... I'd read newspapers and never be able to get past the statistics. I'd watch TV and couldn't see the screen 'cause I'd focus in on the digits on the channel selector.... I'd make love to the wife, and her body would be covered with little numbers, millions of little numbers. Soon, I couldn't even get it up 'til I balanced her debits and credits... *(Shudders.)* I tried to hide it, but people could see. I'd get gunshy around tax season. Start to shake when confronted with a new 'P and L' statement. I knew then I was washed up in the accountancy game... So, I bought a ticket on the first bottle headed for Guttersville, and I've been here ever since...

SIX. And now you don't see the little numbers no more?

TWO. *(Takes a long drink.)* Like hell! They still follow me around. 'Course now I'm too plastered to read the little buggers...

FIVE. What happened to all the..?

TWO. If you'll excuse me, I think I'm going to pass out now....

(He slumps over. The others look at him in disbelief.)

FOUR. Wow... and I always thought accountants were dull...

ONE. Anyone else who wants to share some fascinating story from their past can just forget about it... I don't want scenes from somebody else's pitiful life to flash before my eyes in my last moments.

FIVE. Who said anything about 'last moments?'

ONE. In case you don't remember, we've all been kidnapped at gunpoint.

FOUR. He doesn't look like the kind of guy who would hurt anybody.

ONE. Right. And Jack The Ripper had a really nice smile... Whatta ya think the psycho grabbed us for? Huh? Because he wanted to invite us over for a Christmas Eve slumber party?

FIVE. That doesn't necessarily mean...

ONE. Maybe not in Wimpville. But in real life, we're talking six cases of kidnapping and assault with a deadly weapon. That's life imprisonment if he gets caught. (Grimly.) Remember, each of us has seen his face. If, by some miracle, we do get out of here, any of us could testify against him in court.

SIX. Man's got a point.

ONE. *(To Five.)* So you tell me, Mister 'Expert-On-Human-Behavior...' if you were in that psycho's shoes, would you let any of us live?

(An uncomfortable silence fills the room. Five sees the fear on the faces of the others and tries to rally their spirits.)

FIVE. Actually, this really isn't all that bad.

THREE. What?!

SIX. Are you for real,?

FIVE. To tell the truth, I had no plans for Christmas. Would probably have spent the whole night ringing my bell on some freezing cold street corner. At least this way, I'm with people...

(Another long silence, then...)

FOUR. All I was going to do for Christmas was sit in the forest and meditate.

THREE. Seriously?

FOUR. Well... I did have Call Of Duty and Grand Theft Auto on my iPhone and a case of Red Bull with me.

FIVE. At least that's something.

THREE. Too bad the kidnapper took all our phones.

FIVE. Yeah. Good planning on his part.

FOUR. But Five is right. It is sort of a trip being here. I've never been captured before. Outside of a video game, I mean. And even if you are not exactly the group I might have chosen, it is nice to have company.

(Another, somewhat shorter silence.)

THREE. My Christmas plans were to take sixty pills by eleven and leave this tired old world by midnight. *(Softly.)* I want to thank you guys for talking me out of it.

FIVE. Happy to do it.

THREE. I owe you my life. ... No matter what happens...

(She kisses Five on the cheek.)

ONE. Son of a gun... She's not a lesbian!

THREE. Could you possibly be any more damaged?

ONE. Yeah, well, all that warm and fuzzy might be fine for you guys, but it's not like I had no place to go. The Antelope Lodge is having their annual blowout and I've been looking forward to it all year!

FOUR. The Antelopes?

ONE. Don't knock it. Those guys are a real fraternal organization. That means like brothers.

SIX. Brothers? You mean all your friends are black?

ONE. Hell no. They're buddies, and... *(Embarrassed.)* Uh, you're just pullin' my leg, aren't ya?

SIX. Somebody's got to do it, man. Pullin' your leg is the only way to bring you down to size. And that's the least I can do for my pig-headed amigo.

ONE. You know, Six... I could learn to like you. If you were white and a hell of a lot more like me, that is.

SIX. And I could learn to embarrass myself in public, if I were a hell of a lot more like you, that is.

ONE. Good shot, taco boy.

SIX. Gracias, you pot-bellied, brain-damaged possum-eater.

ONE. *(Grinning.)* You musta read my resume.

(They clink bottles and drink.)

THREE. I'm sorry you had to miss your party, One.

FIVE. Me, too. This isn't that bad for us, since we all had nothing to do and were all alone for the Holidays.

FOUR. Like it's too bad, man.

ONE. Aw, hell... you know, just between us Santas, I been to every Antelope Lodge blowout for the last twenty-six years. I figure I'm about due to miss one.

FOUR. You know something, Santa One? For a redneck, you're okay.

ONE. Thanks. And for a pudding-headed loser, you ain't all that vomit inducing.

FOUR. I choose to take that as a compliment.

FIVE. And speaking for all the whiny, wimpy, wussy boys in the world, I wish you all a Merry Christmas!

TWO. Ditto for the winos!

(They all laugh. Four raises his bottle.)

FOUR. A toast!

TWO. A toast, yeah!

THREE. I need a bottle.

ONE. Here you are, little lady.

THREE. In the spirit of the season... I'm not even going to rip your lungs out for that condescending remark.

ONE. Damn nice of you.

FIVE. So what do we toast to?

FOUR. To a most captive and captivating Christmas!

TWO. Here, here!

ONE. I've bet you been thinking that up all night.

FOUR. Pretty much. Except for the pill-heaving with Three. That was kind of distracting.

(Suddenly, the door suddenly bursts open and Bernie crashes into the room, waving his gun, menacingly. He also carries a stack of gift-wrapped boxes under one arm.)

BERNIE. Stand back! Move away from the door! Move it!

ONE. What's the matter? Couldn't find any more victims?

SIX. Si. Don't you believe in Santas no more?

BERNIE. I don't need anybody else. I got my family now.

FIVE. Family?

ONE. Listen, scumbag. I'd rather have a school of piranhas below the belt than be related to you.

BERNIE. Where's your Christmas spirit?

ONE. *(Surprised.)* Come again?

FOUR. He does have a point there.

SIX. Who's side you on, man?

FOUR. I'm a conscientious protector. I'm on any side that's not gonna get my head blown off.

ONE. You got a backbone of pure Jell-O, you know that?

BERNIE. Okay, everybody gather round. I brought your presents. I know you didn't have time to get me anything. It's okay though.

TWO. Nice of you to be so understanding.

SIX. Hey, the stores are still open, dude. Why don't you, like, let us go and we'll all get you something real nice. Maybe a Prozac gift-pack. Okay?

BERNIE. That's all right. I'm used to not getting any presents at Christmas. Doesn't bother me at all... Well, almost not at all. So don't feel bad. Sit down.

(They don't move. His face darkens and he waves the gun.)

BERNIE. I said, sit down!

(Slowly, they sit on the floor. One stands, staring down the kidnapper with rage and defiance. Bernie pulls back the hammer on the gun pointed at One's head. Neither man flinches. A tense moment.)

SIX.   C'mon, amigo. Do what the happy dude says...

(Slowly, One drops to the floor, never taking his eyes off his captor. As soon as they are all sitting, Bernie sits with a sudden, childlike glee.)

BERNIE.   There! That's better! Isn't it nice to have everyone together? This is the best Christmas I've had in years!

TWO.   *(Burps.)* Don't even make my top fifty.

BERNIE.   Why do you drink so much? It's not good for your health.

ONE.   Why do you kidnap Santa Clauses?

BERNIE.   Why do you complain all the time?

ONE.   We all...

FOUR.   Why are you speaking for all of us? This is a democracy, after all.

ONE.   Why are you such a loser?

THREE.   Why don't you leave him alone?

ONE.   Why don't you swallow some more pills?!

FIVE.   Why are we fighting? Why can't we all just get along?

ONE.   Why don't you shut up, wussy boy!

FIVE.   I was only trying to keep things civilized...

BERNIE.   It's okay. Don't let 'em get to ya. They're always trying to drag you down. *(A strange edge creeps into his voice.)* They always have to make you feel smaller or dumber than they are. Believe me, I know. You can't trust people. You should never trust anyone.

ONE.   Would you like a little paranoia with that whine?

BERNIE.   See what I mean?

FIVE.   Don't mind him. We are all a little on edge here. *(Carefully.)* You do understand why, don't you?

BERNIE. There's no need to be. After all, it's Christmas!

ONE. Can you believe this sh...?!

FIVE. Mind if I ask you a personal question, Mister...uh...?

BERNIE. Call me Bernie.

FIVE. Okay, Bernie... Would you mind if I ask you a question? If it doesn't intrude on your personal feelings that is.

BERNIE. Shoot.

(They all duck.)

BERNIE. I mean... uh, ask me anything.

FIVE. Okay... Bernie... You seem like a nice, reasonable guy...

ONE. Ha!

FIVE. Why would a nice guy like you kidnap six people and lock us in this basement?

BERNIE. *(Shrugs.)* I'm lonely.

FIVE. Well, I'm lonely, too. But that doesn't mean I...

BERNIE. *(Amazed.)* You are?

FIVE. I are...what?

BERNIE. Lonely.

FIVE. Um, sure... I guess.

BERNIE. Wow... Who'da thought?

FIVE. Everybody gets lonely sometimes. It is part of the human condition.

BERNIE. Every one of you?

FIVE. Sure. As a matter of fact, we were just talking about how lonely each of our Christmases were going to be before you...um, invited us here...

BERNIE. So you're saying I did you a favor?

FIVE. I wouldn't exactly put it that way...

BERNIE. But I saved you from having a lonely Christmas, right?

ONE. Now wait a minute! This guy shoves a gun in our faces, locks us in a basement, and Tinkerbell here wants us to write him thank you notes?!

FIVE. Calm down, One. We are just trying to feel our way through Bernie's loneliness issue here.

ONE. I don't feel like talking my way through anything. And don't you lump me in the same group as this space cadet. I'm lonely by choice, not 'cause I'm a fruitcake!

BERNIE. *(Confused.)* Why would anyone choose to be lonely?

TWO. Because he's a fruitcake.

ONE. I didn't mean I was lonely... I meant, well, sometimes, there's, like nobody around to talk to, that's all.

BERNIE. Sometimes?

ONE. So a lot of times! Big deal! It don't mean I'm a psycho like this twisted son of a...

>*(At the mention of the word 'psycho' Bernie leaps to his feet, aiming his gun at One's head.)*

BERNIE. *(Screaming.)* Who's a psycho?! Who you calling a psycho?!

SIX. Chill, man. He didn't mean anything by it... The gringo don't realize how oppressive he can be. But he don't mean anything by it.

ONE. Like hell I don't.

BERNIE. *(Breathing hard.)* Maybe I am a psycho... maybe I am. But it don't give you the right to hate me for it!

ONE. It don't mean I'd let you remove my appendix either.

FIVE. Listen, Mister...

BERNIE. Bernie!

FIVE. Bernie... this is all a lot of fun, but why don't you tell us what it is you really want? Okay?

BERNIE. *(With cold determination.)* I want to play Christmas! That's all. You are all gonna be my family and we're gonna play Christmas. Like it's supposed to be. Like it never was for me... Christmas like that.

FIVE. And that's it? We just play Christmas?

BERNIE. That's it.

FOUR. And then you'll let us go?

(A nervous pause. The tension in the room is unbearable, then...)

BERNIE. I want to play Christmas. That's all. Just Christmas. I've been waiting to play for years... Thinking about it and thinking about it and thinking about it until I knew if I didn't play this year, my head was gonna burst apart. Fly off into bits. And we couldn't let that happen. No, we couldn't let that happen. So we have to play Christmas...

SIX. Dude, if that's all that's got your cajones wired, like no problem. Am I gonna be a wise man or a shepherd? I do a badass shepherd, man.

BERNIE. No. No shepherds. We do this my way. Like the way I've been planning it. The way I rehearsed it over and over and over again.

SIX. What ever gets you your jollies, man. (Sulks.) But I do make a badass shepherd...

(At this sign of compliance, Bernie becomes suddenly childlike again.)

BERNIE. Awesome! Now I'll be the little boy and you be the Mommy.

SIX. Say what?!

ONE. *(Sitting.)* Notice who he didn't ask to be the Mommy? Our Lady of Menswear.

BERNIE. Huh?

THREE. What's that supposed to mean?

FIVE. In all fairness, I think she should be the Mommy.

THREE. Sexist! Just because I'm a woman doesn't mean I'm biologically destined to be a mother!

FIVE. I didn't mean any...

THREE. And just when I thought you were a woke guy!

BERNIE. Hey...

THREE. I insist on being evaluated on my intellectual abilities and not on my ovaries! No one is going to force me into a restrictive role arbitrarily chosen by your perpetually domineering gender to keep us enslaved!

FIVE. That's not what I...

THREE. Motherhood is a choice, not a biological imperative! Women deserve a higher destiny than dirty dishes and disposable diapers!

BERNIE. Hey...

THREE. If you can ever get your filthy minds off of our reproductive organs...

ONE. Heck, I'll be the mother just to shut her up!

THREE. I can't wait until modern technology enables men to give birth, then we all can...

BERNIE. Hey... that Santa's a woman!

TWO. Better not tell her that.

BERNIE. No, really... She's a woman!

ONE. That's still open for debate.

THREE. Stuff it! And as a woman, I demand to be treated with respect, and not have stereotypical occupations thrust upon us in your typical 'man on top' missionary-style society!

ONE. Okay, save the soapbox! Don't be the mother. You'd probably suck at it anyway...

THREE. Oh yeah? I can be as good a mother as any of you. Uh... better!!

BERNIE. *(Confused.)* But... but she's a woman? I didn't know I grabbed a lady Santa.

THREE. Oh? And I suppose you wouldn't have kidnapped me if you knew?

BERNIE. Um, I don't know...

THREE. You see?! That's the kind of sicko sexist sentimentality we have to deal with in this country!

TWO. Mind if I borrow that gun?

THREE. It's almost not worth the breath we waste in arguing with men! Maybe I should just sit down and stop talking and...

(One, Two and Six stand and applaud, preventing her from finishing her sentence. Three sits down in a huff. Five leans over to her, and she slaps his hand away.)

THREE. Don't you even!

BERNIE. *(To One.)* Okay, if she's the mother, you've got to be my old man.

ONE. Uh-uh. No way I play daddy to a degenerate.

BERNIE. *(Raising his gun.)* If you don't be my daddy, I'm gonna blow a new hole in your sinuses.

FOUR. Whoa! Talk about Planned Parenthood.

SIX. Stay cool, dude. Just play the little guy's game and he'll let us go. Okay?

BERNIE. Okay, daddy?

ONE. *(Bitterly.)* Whatever...

BERNIE. Good. *(To Two.)* You can be my uncle Pat. He was in a coma for two years.

TWO. I will do my darnedest to portray the gentleman as besshht I can.

(Two rolls over and passes out again.)

BERNIE. Oh, he's good.

SIX. Must be a method actor.

BERNIE. *(To Four & Five.)* You be my sister, and you be the baby.

ONE. Ha! He sure got a handle on those parts!

FIVE. I've had about enough of you...

BERNIE. The baby can't talk. He can only whine.

ONE. Ha!

FIVE. Now, listen here...

(Bernie aims his pistol at Five and stares him down with wild eyes.)

BERNIE. Baby. Can't. Talk!

FIVE. Uh... goo goo goo...

BERNIE. And since she's gonna be the Mommy. That makes you the butler.

SIX. The butler?!

BERNIE. So we were well off. So kill me.

SIX. Kill you? I ain't even talking to you, man! Go lay your white-assed power trips on some other oppressed minority.

BERNIE. *(Impressed.)* Wow. that's exactly what our butler used to say... Now, here are all your presents. *(Hands them each a gift.)* Butler... Uncle... Sister... Baby... Mom... *(Coldly.)* And we can't forget Dad. No we can never forget Dad. *(Smiling.)* And here we are! One big happy family!

FOUR. Yeah. A real Hallmark moment.

ONE. Tell me, Mother-dear. Why couldn't you have had an abortion?

THREE. Because they were probably illegal at the time, Father-dear. Thanks to your all-male Supreme Court!

TWO. Does like everything have to be a big political issue with you?

THREE. What do you mean?

FIVE. I think what he means is that your speechifying is getting... well, kind of old...

TWO. The pyramids are old... That line is just plain boring.

THREE. Boring? You find issues of equality boring?!

SIX. The way you carry on and on about it, we do. I'm just glad you're not on the side of us minorities. One speech from you could set civil rights back a few hundred years.

THREE. You all think I'm boring?

FIVE. Not exactly boring... more like, well, tedious to the extreme.

THREE. *(Stunned.)* Tedious to the extreme?

FIVE. But in a good way! *(Gently.)* All I'm saying is that, maybe if you toned down the preaching a bit, people might find it easier to listen to what you had to say.

THREE. Me? Preach? Did you hear that? This man said I preach!

ONE, TWO, FOUR & SIX. Amen!

THREE. *(Embarrassed.)* Uh, okay, so maybe I do get carried away sometimes... It's only that I don't want any of you to think you can take advantage of me. Because I'm a woman, I mean.

FIVE. No one is going to take advantage of you, Three. You are among friends here.

BERNIE. Family!

FOUR. Yeah... Family.

FIVE. We'll treat you like one of the guys, I promise.

THREE. Thanks. uh... I'm sorry if I've been... tedious.

TWO. To the extreme...

FIVE. It's all right.

FOUR. Like no problemo.

BERNIE. We all love you, Mom. Don't we, Dad?

ONE. Shut up, psycho.

(Bernie leaps up and brandishes his pistol. He aims it at One.)

BERNIE. Did you call me psycho again?! I heard it! I heard him call me psycho! I'm gonna put a big fat bullet right in your big fat head!

ONE. I, uh... didn't say psycho. I said... shut up... uh, son. Let me read my paper, okay?

(Bernie sits again, suddenly calm.)

BERNIE. *(Rambling.)* Sure. Okay... My old man, he used to spend hours reading the newspaper. That's all you used to do. You loved the paper... Sometimes you would roll it up with the comics page on the outside...and then if I got in your way, you'd swat me across the mouth and laugh and said it wouldn't hurt as much with the funny papers on the outside. *(Rubs his cheek.)* But I never noticed the difference...

FOUR. That's funny. My Pop used to do the same thing. With the comics, I mean.

FIVE. My Dad had a leather strap with our names on it.

ONE. *(Uncomfortably.)* Maybe you deserved it.

FIVE. Usually we did...

BERNIE. *(Cheerfully.)* Hey! It's time to open up presents. You go first, Uncle!

(He unwraps a bottle of fine French wine, and inspects the label)

TWO. Hey! This is a Lafitte-Rothschilde, 1967! After twelve years of Thunderbird, this'll be like heaven! Thanks, kid. You made my Christmas.

BERNIE. You're welcome, uncle. You can go pass out now.

TWO. *(Rolling over.)* I'll do my best.

BERNIE. It's your turn, Butler.

(Six eagerly tears into his package and pulls out a gold pocket watch.)

SIX. Hey! Check it! It looks like real gold! *(Puts it to his ear.)* It even runs!

BERNIE. Of course it runs. And it's real gold. That's a family heirloom. My old man left it to me.

SIX. You sure you want me to have it? I mean, you don't owe me nothin', little strange dude.

BERNIE. You used to play with me a lot when I was growing up. You were the only one who seemed to notice I was alive. It's the only thing I can do to thank you. *(Tears in his eyes.)* It's yours now, butler... Merry Christmas.

SIX. Gracias, amigo! I always wanted a gold pocket watch. Now all I need are pockets. You're all right, little dude.

BERNIE. *(To Five.)* It's your turn, baby brother. Need any help opening it?

(He helps Five unwrap the present, which turns out to contain...)

FIVE. A rattle?

ONE. Hahahaha!

BERNIE. *(As if talking to a baby.)* You're only one-and-a-half. And it's a really good rattle. I made it myself from wood. None of that plastic crap for my baby brother. No, only the best!

FIVE. Imagine my excitement.

BERNIE. Sssssh. You are too young to talk. Now wrap your little hands around it like this. Come on!

FIVE. Give me a break, I...

BERNIE. *(Leaping up.)* I said you're too young to talk! You hear me?! Babies can't talk! I won't let them! You hear me?! I won't let them! Are you gonna talk or what?!

(Everybody is stunned by the sudden insanity, and the intensity of his ravings. They are reminded of how dangerous this situation really is. A tense pause, then...)

FIVE. Uh... gurgle gurgle goo?

BERNIE. *(Cheerful again.)* That's a good baby. Now grab it and shake it! That's it. Shake! What a good boy you are. Not like your older brother. No. Your older brother worries people. He scares them. But you, you're a good boy.

FOUR. He does have a talent for it. Can I open mine now, bro?

BERNIE. Sure, Sis.

(Four tears open the present to reveal a small Latex disk.)

FOUR. Awesome! A mini Frisbee.

THREE. That's no Frisbee. That's a diaphragm! What kind of guy would buy something like that for his sister? That's disgusting!

ONE. He's your son.

BERNIE. *(Icily.)* I think it's time you opened your present, Daddy.

ONE. Oh, all right.

>   *(The gruff Santa slowly shreds the wrapping paper. He opens the box, leaps to his feet and screams, flinging the box and its gruesome contents across the room.)*

ONE. Aaaarrrgghh! That's sick... that's really sick...

THREE. What is it? What's wrong?

BERNIE. *(Giggling.)* You like your gift, don't you, Daddy?

FIVE. What was in the box, One?

ONE. A rat... A bloody rat. Shot through the head.

>   *(And the realization hits them all.)*

THREE. Oh, my God...

>   *(The crazed kidnapper stands and slowly raises his gun. He aims it at Santa One, as the lights dim.)*

CURTAIN

End of Act Two

ACT THREE

AT RISE. Moments later. The curtain opens to the same scene as the end of Act Two. Santa One glares with hatred, as the deranged kidnapper aims his pistol at the older man's head. The others look on in horror.)

BERNIE. *(Breathing hard.)* You like it, Daddy? Did you like your present?!

ONE. A dead rat. That's real sick, you know that?! Real sick. They outa put you away for good!

BERNIE. They tried that. They tried, but I got out... I fooled them good. All of them.

(Bernie's eyes narrow with insane cruelty.)

BERNIE. I waited... I waited years. Years, to get you back. All those things you did to me. The beatings... locking me in the cellar... And the time, most of all I remember, the time... the time I was putting the star on top of the Christmas tree... I was putting the star up and the ladder slipped, so I hung there on to the top of that skinny Christmas tree... feeling my little legs step on nothing but air. Scared... So scared 'cause I was so little, and the tree was so high, and I was standing on nothing. So I screamed for you to help me.... Please, please help me, Daddy... And you came and looked at me hanging in the tree, and then...then you laughed. You laughed!! *(Regressing to the little child.)* You said to jump, and you'd catch me. Jump, Bernie, you said... I was so scared, and you told me to jump, and I was so little, and you were my Daddy, so I jumped...

(Bernie winces, as if he can feel the impact, even today.)

BERNIE. Only you didn't catch me. You didn't catch me! And as I lay there, all scrunched up on the living room floor, just lying there crying and screaming and not understanding... you looked down at me and said... "That'll teach you not to trust anyone." You said, "Trusting other people will only cause you pain!" And I learned, Daddy. I learned real good. Never trust anyone... Never trust anyone... And I never ever let anybody hurt me again, Daddy. Not without me hurting them first. You taught me that.

(He pulls back the firing pin with a loud, "klitch-clack.")

BERNIE. And after all these years… I finally get a chance to teach you a lesson, too!

FIVE. Put the gun down, Bernie… Just put the gun down…

THREE. Don't hurt him! Please! Don't hurt him!

FOUR. Yeah, man. He's not your father!

SIX. He's not the one you gotta get even with.

FOUR. You don't even know him, man. He never did anything to you. Your old man did all that, not this guy!

FIVE. That's right… Hate your father, Bernie, not him!

ONE. Shut up, all of you!

BERNIE. See?! He's talking just like my old man! Shut up was all he ever said to me! Shut up!

FIVE. Easy, One. We need to be calm to defuse this situation.

ONE. Defuse, nothing! You know something, psycho? I'm sick and tired of all your whining about how cruel your Daddy was… It'd almost be worth it for you to shoot me, just so's they'd lock you up for good!

FIVE. One!

ONE. I'm sick to death of the whole world complaining about how cruel or stupid or not there their old man was. Daytime talk shows, Internet pity parties, support groups and all that other psychotherapist bullshit… I'm sick of it. You think it's easy being a father? Sure, all he's gotta do is be strong and shout orders, right? Well, you try it sometime. You try shouting orders when you're dying inside. When you get laid off and got no idea how to pay the rent that month or put food on the table. You try it. Try to help with your kid's homework when your wife is sleeping around and you have to hide it from the kids…You see what that feels like! You can't ever let your guard down when you're a Dad. Because you're the man of the house, the bread-winner, the one who's supposed to have all the answers. And there's always some snot-nosed little rodent looking up to you…needing you to be strong… Even when you know you're not…

(His eyes glaze over, as he speaks to someone from long ago.)

ONE.   ...and that little guy can't handle you breaking down. He'd be scared to death to see you cry... Because if Dad can't handle it, who can? If you crack, what's gonna stop the kid from cracking, too? You're all he got. And you gotta be strong for him, no matter what... *(Gritting his teeth.)* So you show that little soldier nothing's wrong. Nothin's stronger than Dad...

(The others are silent. One seems even further away now.)

ONE.   *(Softer.)* And no matter what, you can't help but love the little vermin, 'cause he loves his father, even if you never asked him to...It's in their genes, like being born with a big nose, or black hair or something, and you can't help but love him back....Until one day, he's fifteen and just found out that it's not cool anymore to love your Dad. He just found out that anybody who is anybody has an attitude, and an old man he can't stand to be on the same planet with... *(With growing anger.)* So this kid you'd take a bullet for...he walks through the door and you stupidly stand there thinking nothing's changed...That he's still the same little boy you played ball with even when you were dead-tired after a whole week of gettin' your ass chewed out at some job you hate... You think he's the same little guy you helped with his science project, even though you knew next to nothin' about it yourself... That he's the same little boy you packed off to school that morning, and a thousand other mornings before that, because Mom was still out who-knows-where, doing who-knows-what with who-knows-who...So you move to hug him, like you hugged him every day since he was a baby, even when he had a full diaper or spit up, you still hugged him because he's more important than any shirt or shoes. And he has to know so he's loved and special... (Confused, hurt.) ...Only this time, he backs away...He backs away and stares at you with that look...that look that stops you dead in your tracks....And he lets you know without saying a word, that you can never hug your son again...that he's not your little boy any more, and he doesn't need you to worry about him or protect him or even love him anymore, because he's way too cool for that now... He gives you that look that says, it don't matter what you've done or sacrifiied or cried over all these years. You are irrelevant in his life.

MORE

ONE. His image and the friends he just met are way more important than you. He throws you that look that says it's over. You're done. He doesn't need you or want you in his life anymore. *(With pain.)* So you hit him…You hit him for all the times you wanted to cry, but held back for his sake, and now he goes and makes you feel worse than any of those other times. And you go to hit him again…*(Frightened.)* Only this time, you realize what you've done, and you catch you're hand in mid-air…But it's too late. The sound of that first slap is still echoing in both your ears. And his look is as cold and hateful as anything you've ever seen in your life. And the next thing you know, he's run off to live with his mother and this week's lover of hers and…and…and… *(Weakly.)* So you just try bein' a father…just try… Because that's all a Dad can do…is try…

(He slumps down against the wall, his back to the others, his body wracked by silent tears.)

ONE. *(Without turning to face them.)* … So you do what you have to do, boy. Shoot me in the back if you want. You can't possibly hurt me anymore than you already have…

(Bernie's finger twitches on the trigger, but he can't get himself to fire. Santa One turns, looks at him with a sorrowful empty expression. He nods, then exits through the curtain, Stage Right. In the ensuing tension, Santa Three walks over to Bernie, who still stands pointing the gun where his surrogate father was standing.)

THREE. How could you do that to him?

BERNIE. I didn't… I…

THREE. How could you do that to your own father?!

BERNIE. I didn't mean to… I didn't know he felt like that… I didn't know he had any feelings at all!

THREE. You should be ashamed of yourself.

BERNIE. I didn't know, Mommy!

THREE. You are lucky to have a father like him. You all are!

BERNIE. Stop talking to me like that. He's… he's not my father. He's not even Santa Claus!

FIVE. That does it! I've had about enough from you.

>   *(Caught up in their own tortured memories, they all bear in on the crazy man with the gun.)*

BERNIE. Stay back!

SIX. Man. I'm tired of you hurting good people.

TWO. Yeah, you little punk!

BERNIE. I didn't mean to. Look! I still have the gun! I'm still dangerous!

TWO. *(Sarcastically.)* Oh, yeah. Big man with a gun…

THREE. You're an ungrateful brat. You always were.

FIVE. You always got all of Dad's attention. He never even noticed me. But you, you were the oldest and you could never do anything wrong!

BERNIE. What are you talking about? Huh? You're crazy!

FIVE. You got all the attention. All the breaks. And you were the one who hurt Mom and Dad the most!

BERNIE. What are you talking about? I don't even know you! Any of you!

FIVE. All you ever did was take advantage of everyone who was ever good to you!

BERNIE. I'm not your brother, man! You're acting crazy! Stay back or I'll shoot…!

FIVE. Give me that thing!

>   *(Santa Five snatches the gun out of Bernie's hand like it was a toy.)*

FIVE. Now get out of here before I kick your butt like I should've done twenty years ago!

>   *(Bernie is stunned, standing in a room with no gun and surrounded by a mob of angry Santa Clauses. He hesitates, then runs from the room.*

FIVE. And don't even think about coming back!

>   *(The others look at Five with newfound respect.)*

TWO. *(Slapping him on the back.)* You're a good kid, you know that?

THREE. You grabbed the gun right out of his hand. That was the single bravest thing I ever saw!

SIX. Whoa! Ain't nobody gonna call you wussy boy no more!

FOUR. That was so awesome, dude! When you said to that psycho, "Don't come back," and he...

FIVE. *(Sudden realization.)* Don't come back?! What did I do?!

(Five runs to the door. It's locked. He's stunned.)

FIVE. Don't come back... I told him to leave and not come back...How can I be such an idiot?

(Five crumples to the floor, as Santa Three walks over and puts a consoling hand on his shoulder.)

FIVE. How could I be so stupid..?

THREE. It was still a beautiful thing you did...

(Santa One enters through the Stage Right curtain. He scans the silent group. No kidnapper in sight.)

ONE. What's going on? Where's the psycho?

FOUR. You should have seen it! Five, here, took Bernie's gun and threw him out!

FIVE. *(Moaning.)* I told him to not even think about coming back...

ONE. Hey, that's great!

FIVE. But I forgot he could lock the door again...

ONE. You *what?!!*

FIVE. I'm sorry...

ONE. You took the kidnapper's gun, invited him to leave, and then let him lock the door again?!

FIVE. I guess I got a little carried away, with you being our Dad and all, and my brother breaking your heart all over again...

ONE. You're a wussy boy, you know that?!

THREE. Leave him alone. He did it for you.

ONE. He left us trapped in here for me?

SIX. Yeah. Like he saw you as his Daddy and risked his life backing you up.

ONE. Yeah?

SIX. It was a real superhero moment, man! Like Spiderman or Hulk throwing down! You would'a been proud.

FIVE. I'm sorry, One. I screwed up again.

ONE. *(Softening.)* Aw... hell. It's okay.

FIVE. You mean it?

ONE. You can't go through your whole life trying to win my approval. Look what that did to the psycho...

FIVE. I guess...

ONE. Besides. You got the gun now and we can shoot the lock off.

TWO. That's right!

FOUR. I always wanted to see someone do that!

(One takes the pistol from Five and points it towards the steel door.)

ONE. Okay, everybody! Get behind me. The bullets might ricochet!

(They all take cover behind the big man with the gun.)

ONE. Here goes!

(With a wince, he squeezes the trigger three times. Nothing.)

FOUR. I don't think it ricocheted...

ONE. It didn't fire, stupid!

FIVE. Empty?

ONE. *(Checking the gun.)* Empty.
(One throws the gun in the corner and they all sit dejectedly.)

ONE. So much for being home by New Year's...

FIVE. Or ever...

(Six looks at the sad Santas. A smile comes over his face.)

SIX. You know what I miss the most?

FOUR. What?

SIX. Christmas dinner... My Rosa, she's the best cook on the block. It doesn't matter how many pennies you have to save all year long, how many candy bars for lunch... come Christmas, my Rosa goes all out!

FIVE. Now that you mention it, I am pretty hungry.

FOUR. I'm starving!

TWO. Why would anyone wanna waste good wine by putting food in their stomach?

FIVE. One?

ONE. Yeah.

FIVE. I'm really sorry.

ONE. It's okay, kid. You didn't know.

THREE. I guess we all have shadows in our past that refuse to let us go... no matter how in control of our lives we think we are.

SIX. You said it, sister.

(They sit quietly, reflecting on their lives. Slowly, the steel door creaks open. No one even jumps up as Bernie enters with another gun.)

ONE. Back for another round of *Christmas With The Crazies*?

BERNIE. Uh.. I just wanted to tell you...

ONE. *(Standing.)* You expect us to be afraid? That gun empty too?

(Bernie FIRES at One's feet. They all jump back.)

TWO. My guess would be 'no.'

BERNIE. *(Hesitantly.)* I just wanted to say... I'm sorry for making you cry.

ONE. That'll be the day you make me cry, sicko.

BERNIE. Yeah, well. I...I didn't mean to... I guess sometimes fathers mess up as much as kids do.

ONE. There ain't exactly an all-purpose college course for being a Daddy. It's sort of on-the-job training.

TWO. And some people flunk out.

FIVE. And do damage.

ONE. Yeah. Sometimes we flunk out and do damage. But most of the time, we're tryin' to do the best we can... It's a hell of a thing, not knowing for eighteen years or more whether you done a good job or not. *(Softly.)* And by that time... it's too late to do anything but feel bad about it...

BERNIE. I'm sorry.

ONE. If you're waiting for me to say thanks for apologizing... don't hold your breath.

BERNIE. I won't.

(Bernie releases a staccato breath. This is difficult for him.)

BERNIE. I...I wanted you all to know that... that this was all new to me. Not just kidnapping Santas, but all of it. See, I didn't know. I thought I was the only one who hurt. With memories that scar and sear your thoughts 'til you can only scream, until there's nothing left inside to cry out your eyes... You grab your stomach and rock back and forth, begging God to let you die, with guilt and loneliness crumpling you up like food poisoning... And, I... I thought I was the only one who hurt like that.

ONE. Yeah... well, welcome to the planet, kid.

BERNIE. Um... I know I can never make this all up to you, missin' your Christmas and everything...but... but I... *(Shoulders slump.)* Well, anyway... Merry Christmas...

(He turns and exits. The steel door clanks loudly behind him.)

ONE. *(Under his breath.)* Merry Christmas to you too, psycho...

FOUR. It's funny, but I kinda feel sorry for the little guy. I guess when people are always labeling you a loser or a freak, you learn to sympathize with those who really earn the title.

THREE. I get that.

FIVE. So here we are, right back where we started. I think we can assume that Bernie won't be coming back any time soon.

THREE. If ever.

FOUR. Which brings us back to the subject of food.

SIX. Hey, has anyone looked in any of those boxes back there?

TWO. We did find the wine... Thank heavens.

FIVE. Six is right. We might as well scrounge around to see if we can find something to eat. Maybe the psycho stuffed something away in some of these boxes.

(They all begin picking through the boxes with little enthusiasm. They pull out odd props - rubber chickens, strange clothing, broken toys, etc.)

FIVE. Some of this stuff is pretty bizarre. Take a look at these.

(He holds up a set of Mickey Mouse ears.)

FOUR. Mickey Mouse ears! Outrageous. Can I wear them?

FIVE. Knock yourself out. Merry Christmas, Four.

FOUR. Thanks, Five. Wait a minute, I saw something in the other room.

ONE. Hope it was a shower.

(Four exits through the Stage Right curtain. He re-enters carrying a large framed photo of Donald Trump. Hands it to Santa One.)

FOUR. This is for you, One. Merry Christmas!

ONE. Donald Trump... Gee, thanks. That's really, you know, touching.

TWO. Let me look, too!

(As the others continue scrounging, Two walks through the steel door, and continues off-stage. Five is the first to see the door open.)

FIVE. Two!!

TWO. *(Offstage.)* I haven't found anything yet!

FIVE. The door. It's unlocked!

TWO. *(Entering.)* 'Course it is. I couldn't walk through if it was, Four... I mean, Three... Or are you Five? *(Shaking his head)* And I used to be so good with numbers...

FOUR. We're free!

TWO. Huh? Oh, I get it... Hey, everybody! The door is unlocked!

(They all jump up and dash for the door.)

ONE. Let's get outta here!

SIX. Rosalita, I'm coming home for Christmas!

THREE. Wait, One!

ONE. What for?

THREE. Uh.. don't forget your Trump.

(She hesitantly hands him the framed photo of Trump.)

ONE. Oh, yeah. Uh, thanks.

(He smiles at her awkwardly, wanting to say more than he is able to express. Then turns and exits through the steel door.)

FIVE. *(Waving after them.)* Merry Christmas, you guys!

FOUR. *(Offstage.)* Merry Christmas, Santa man!

(A pause, as Three and Five are left alone on stage.)

FIVE. Looks like it's just us.

THREE. I, uh.. guess we should be going, too.

FIVE. I guess.

(Pause. Neither one moves.)

THREE. By the way... I'd like to thank you for saving my life... twice.

FIVE. My pleasure.

THREE. No. I really mean it.

FIVE. Look, this may sound like a line, and don't kick my butt for saying it... *(Looks deep into her eyes)* ...it was really nice meeting you. All things considered.

THREE. *(Hesitantly.)* It was nice meeting you, too.

FIVE. I even didn't mine holding your hair when you threw up in that bucket.

THREE. You sure know how to sweet talk a woman.

(An uncomfortable pause, then...)

FIVE. *(Simultaneously.)* Would you like..?

THREE. *(Simultaneously.)* How about if we..? *(Pauses, then smiles.)* After you.

FIVE. Ladies first. *(Winces.)* Um, sorry. I'll try to stop saying things like that.

THREE. It's okay... I was just going to ask if you would like to spend the rest of the holiday together? I mean, seeing that you're not all that obnoxiously male. And since neither of us have any plans, and we've been through a certain ordeal together... and...

FIVE. And...?

THREE. ...and to tell the truth, I hadn't figured on living out the day, so my calendar is somewhat open.

FIVE. How could I resist an invitation like that?

(They look deeply into each other's eyes, that slowly melts into a tender kiss. Five pulls away, bubbling with excitement.)

FIVE. Did you ever get the feeling, you know, how things turn out so sappy sometimes, that you're living in an old black and white movie?

THREE. No.

FIVE. *(Embarrassed.)* Oh... well, I don't either. So where do you want to go?

THREE. How about my place for dinner? No. We, uh, better make it yours. I already called the utility company and told them to turn off the gas and electricity.

FIVE. You really prepared, didn't you?

THREE. I guess when you spend your whole life waiting for bad things to happen, you tend to lose sight of the good things around you.

FIVE. Maybe I can help you find them again. I'm an eternal optimist.

THREE. Maybe I can cure you of that.

FIVE. May the strongest neurosis win.

THREE. You're on... Shall we go? *(Suddenly stops.)* Wait a second. My beard.

(She picks up her beard and puts it on.)

FIVE. You know something? I've never seen you with a beard.

THREE. You like?

FIVE. It may take a bit getting used to.

THREE. *(An invitation.)* I've got time.

(They walk to the door, smiling. He takes her hand in his.)

FIVE. Me, too. *(Stops suddenly.)* You know, come to think of it... I don't even know your name. Santa Three won't do forever.

THREE. I'm sort of embarrassed to tell you... My real name is...

OFFSTAGE VOICE. Where do you two think you're going?!

FIVE. He's back! Hide!

(They duck behind the boxes, just as Santa Four pops his head through the door.)

FOUR. Cool your jets, dude and dudette. It's only us.

FIVE. What are you doing back here?

FOUR. *(Entering.)* Well, we called the police to pick up the kidnapper, and they said he already turned himself in. After that, we figured we'd head on back for Christmas Dinner. *(To the door.)* Maestro?

(Six enters carrying a large McDonald's Hamburger bag. One and Two follow, carrying smaller bags.)

TWO. Tada!

ONE.   Merry Christmas, wussy boy. Butch girl.

FIVE.   But what about Rosa's Christmas dinner?

SIX.   I thought I told you. Rosa is manager of the McDonald's down the street. Wait 'til you taste her french fries, amigo. She makes the best fries in the whole world.

FIVE.   I don't believe it...

THREE.   They do say this is the season for miracles.

(They all crouch down in a circle and divide up the food.)

FOUR.   Dibs on the chocolate shake!

FIVE.   Listen, guys... I was thinking. If Bernie turned himself in... he must have intentionally left the door unlocked... it seems a shame he has to...

ONE.   *(Munching a burger.)* Way ahead of you, Fiver. We already decided to go down to the police station and tell them we're not pressing charges... as long as the psycho agrees to check himself in for some counseling. Serious counseling.

FOUR.   Mega counseling.

THREE.   One, I'm surprised at you! You really are a sweetheart.

(She kisses him on the cheek. He grimaces and swats her away.)

ONE.   Hey! I'm not back two minutes and she's already treating me like a sex object! You know how demeaning it is to be seen as nothing more than a piece of meat?!

THREE.   *(Smacking his head, happily.)* Shut up, you reactionary jerk.

ONE.   I'll forgive you for that...if you pass me another burger.

THREE.   I see how you got that Santa belly.

FOUR.   Don't forget. Mine is the Veggieburger.

ONE.   Why the heck can't you gnaw on animal flesh like a normal person?

FOUR.   You call eating something that moos and poops in a field normal?

ONE.   Don't get me started!

FIVE.   Does red wine go with cheeseburgers?

TWO.   Any wine goes with anything. It's the quantity that's important.

SIX.   Hey, save some fries for me, man!

THREE.   Fight you for it, home boy.

>   *(The lights dim as they all lunge for the food bags.)*

CURTAIN

The End

About The Playwright

Vin Morreale, Jr. is an internationally produced playwright, published author and award-winning screenwriter.

Vin was a founding member of the San Francisco Playwrights Center and the Senseless Bickering Comedy Theatre. He has directed hundreds of works for stage, screen and radio across the country. He was awarded the prestigious *Al Smith Writing Fellowship*, and his scripts, stage plays, documentaries, museum exhibits and radio comedy have received hundreds of productions around the world, as well as being translated into Chinese, Italian, Russian and Spanish.

Vin has sold material to network and cable television networks, had screenplays optioned and produced, and his work has been seen in more than 15 countries. He was named a top screenwriter by both The International Screenwriters Association and TheBlacklist.org.

As president of *Vin Morreale Casting,* along with his nationally known *Burning Up The Stage* acting workshops, he has helped nearly 30,000 actors find work in movies, TV, stage and video.

You can find more of his books and plays at *academyartspress.com*.

VIN MORREALE, JR.

Also by Vin Morreale, Jr.

ACADEMY ARTS PRESS
http://academyartspress.com/shop-for-books

The KISS ME Curse
The Carrie Variations
Forsaken
All My Passions
300 Monologues
Two Character Chaos
150 Acting Scenes
Chicken Fat For The Damaged Psyche
Knowing When To Leave
Dark Wilderness & Other Stories
Mabel The Maple
Too Many Rules

DRAMATIC PUBLISHING
dramaticpublishing.com/authors/profile/view/url/vin-morreale-jr

Burning Up The Stage – *Monologues & Audition Scenes for Actors from 6 to 70*
Breaking & Entering
House of The Seven Gables
Uncool
Nicky's Secret
Southern Discomfort
The Happy Holidays Collection

ELDRIDGE PUBLISHING
histage.com/search?q=Morreale

The Fairyland Detective Agency
Sonoma White & The Seven Dots
Fairies, Fantasies & Just Plain Fun

OFF THE WALL PUBLISHING
offthewallplays.com

Exquisite Anxieties – Seven Slivers Of Suspense
Temp Work
Empathy – A Celebration Of Women's Voices
Ladies Guild Pre-Christmas Planning Session